## CWO
## Anthony "Tony" Alleyne
### (U.S. Navy Retired)

# SURROUNDED

# BY

# WATER

*Island Stories ...*

*Life on Three Islands*

# CWO ANTHONY 'TONY' ALLEYNE (U.S. NAVY RETIRED)

## Surrounded By Water

*Island Stories... Life on Three Islands*

*DEDICATION*

*To my mother, whose love anchored my life and whose strength
guided me through every storm.
To my family, who supported me even when the sea called me far
from home.
To my mentors and shipmates, who believed in me, challenged me,
and helped shape the sailor and the man I became.
My life story is because of you.*

"Mastering one's life isn't just about living; it's about embracing the experience."

— Anthony A. Alleyne

# Contents

# Preface

Every life is a journey not just across time and distance, but through the places, people, and lessons that shape who we become. My journey began in Harlem, on the island of Manhattan, where bustling city streets taught me resilience and ambition. It continued in the towns of Chilmark and Oak Bluffs, on the island of Martha's Vineyard, where I discovered identity, community, and purpose. It brought me to the town of Wailuku on the island of Maui, where reflection and peace showed me what it truly means to live.

Each of these islands is a chapter of my story, a shore that taught me something new about who I am. Along the way, I served twenty-five years in the United States Navy, a life defined by saltwater and steel, discipline and discovery. From the decks of ships and the roar of jets catapulting, to quiet moments behind a camera lens, the sea carried me farther than I ever imagined and always brought me home.

This memoir is more than a record of places and dates. It is a story of transformation: from a boy in Harlem to a sailor navigating the world's oceans. From a photographer documenting history to a son returning home to care for his mother. From a man searching for meaning to one who finds it in the rhythm of the tides.

I share these stories not only as a record of where I have been, but as a reflection of the people and places that shaped me. They are stories of challenges and triumphs, of laughter and loss, of duty and devotion. Above all, they are stories of how the sea and the islands have defined the course of my life.

I hope as you read these pages, you see not just one man's journey but echoes of your own, the people who anchored you, the places that changed you, and your own unique life experiences. Because in the end, we are all, in one way or another, surrounded by water.

*Anthony "Tony" Alleyne*
  *Maui, Hawaii*
  *January 2026*

# Acknowledgments

This book would not have been possible without the love, encouragement, and guidance of many people who shaped my journey.

To my mother, whose strength, courage, and unwavering belief in me carried me farther than I ever imagined. Thank you for anchoring my life with love.

To my family and friends, who supported me through deployments, homecomings, and every chapter in between. Your presence gave meaning to each step of the journey.

To my shipmates, mentors, and leaders throughout my twenty-five years in the United States Navy, thank you for the lessons, the laughter, and the lifelong bonds forged at sea.

Also, the many people who shared stories, offered guidance, or inspired me along the way, this memoir is as much yours as it is mine.

A tremendous amount of appreciation to my high-school coach and lifelong mentor, Coach Jay Schofield, teacher, author, and friend, whose words of encouragement on and off the course helped shape both the runner I became and the writer I am today. His belief in clarity, rhythm, and purpose continues to guide my stride, on the page and in life.

Finally, thank you to the islands that became a part of me, each shaping who I am. This story reflects them all.

# Advance Reader Feedback

*"Tony Alleyne's book gently grabbed me by the hand right from the Preface and led me through a powerful, well-written memoir of his life, **Surrounded By Water**. It was an interesting, intriguing, easy read that flowed until the end."*
— **A. Pocknett**

*"WOW, a compelling narrative that masterfully connects a journey across Manhattan, Martha's Vineyard, and Maui. Honest, heartfelt reflections make the story profoundly relatable."*
— **TC Lee**

# Part I

*Harlem Beginnings*

# 1

# Chapter 1

Harlem Beginnings

*~ A vibrant island tethered to the mainland by bridges, ferries, and tunnels*

Harlem was a predominantly Black neighborhood on the island of Manhattan, New York. This is the first island where my story begins. The year was 1952. I was born at Sloan Medical Center for Women. My earliest memories are filled with the sounds, smells, and rhythms of a bustling neighborhood that was alive at every hour of the day, hearing street vendors bellowing "Wateee Mellon" from their carts. The Mister Softee ice cream jingle could be heard two blocks away, while keen competition was fierce from the Good Humor ice cream trucks. Neighbors stood on their stoops talking about everything and playing their daily numbers when the numbers runner would swing by. All while others kept a watchful eye from apartments above. Harlem wasn't just where I grew up; it was where I played and felt safe, and where every grown-up could discipline anyone's child. That was my community.

Harlem was the home of numerous influential musicians, writers, activists, and politicians. They included: Duke Ellington, Harry Belafonte, Maya Angelou, Langston Hughes, Malcom X, James Baldwin, Adam Clayton Powell, and Thurgood Marshall.

Before I took my first breath, my family had already known loss. An older brother was born, but he only lived a few days and never left the hospital. Though I never knew him, that quiet absence shaped my family in ways I only came to understand later. My parents, Audrey and Gladstone Alleyne, poured their love and hopes into my sister, Vanessa, and me to build a life that moved forward.

We lived in a three-bedroom apartment on the fifth floor, 501 West 143rd Street. Our building was on the corner of Amsterdam Avenue and Hamilton Place, on the Upper West Side of Manhattan. A place that felt like the center of the world to me. Outside our apartment building, on the streets below, there was a barbershop where men conversed, and B.S.'d the news of the day, a bank where neighbors cashed their paychecks, a Rexall drugstore across the street, and a small Puerto Rican bodega store. Life was close-knit and connected, each person part of a larger fabric woven from shared struggles, dreams, and hopes.

Just two blocks away, on 145th Street, was P.S. 186, my first school. It was an easy walk from our apartment. I still remember the sound of taps coming from my shoes, echoing on the sidewalk as I walked in the mornings. Not far beyond stood the RKO movie theater on Broadway between 145th and 146th Street, where Saturday matinees cost just fifty cents for a double feature. On my way, I'd walk past the Thom McCann shoe store, grab a slice of the best New York pizza for a quarter, and sometimes stop by the Chinese restaurant where my father would buy Egg Foo Young to bring home for dinner. Those small routines, the smell of the pizza, the taste of the Egg Foo Young, and the glow of the theater marquee are etched in my memory as clearly as any photograph I would ever take.

Family church attendance was a must for my mother. I was baptized, confirmed to receive Communion, and served as an Acolyte at the Chapel of the Intercession, an Episcopal church. The grounds took up two city blocks from 155th Street and Amsterdam Avenue down to Broadway, continuing to Riverside Drive. One entire block was a cemetery, while the other consisted of more cemetery grounds, a huge Gothic-style Church, and Rectory. The church was quite notable, serving as the final resting place of Clement Clarke Moore, the author of the famous poem "The Night Before Christmas."

One Sunday morning, around 8:30 am, I was heading to church by train. While waiting at the 145th Street subway station, I was approached by three kids about my age who wanted my church money. The station was empty, no one was around, I was about to being mugged. My back was against the wall with the three kids semi-circled around me. Nervous and scared, I could only run. I pushed my way through them and ran as hard and fast as I could. New York subway stations are a maze. I managed to get myself to the opposite side of the station just as a train was coming. I jumped on the train, which is ten cars long, and managed to get away from the would-be muggers. I got off two stations later, crossed over to catch the next train, and made it to church. After church, I walked back home from 155th Street to 143rd Street. That was one of those days you never forget.

My parents both worked hard to give my sister and me the best life they could. My mother, Audrey, was determined and driven. She started as a bank teller. Through perseverance and sheer will, rose to become head teller at The First National City Bank of New York, built in 1927 on Broadway and Canal Street. I remember how proud I was watching her put on makeup in the morning, knowing she was building a financial future for us. My father, Gladstone, a World War II Veteran, worked for the U.S. Postal Service at night, sorting mail on the trains that ran from Grand Central Station to Connecticut. It was demanding work, but he did it with pride, and it gave me an early lesson in dedication and responsibility.

What I remember most about those early years was the sense of belonging. Hot summer days, boys playing Stickball, Skellez, or Crack the Top in the street, while girls jumped Double-Dutch on the sidewalk. Older folks sat around watching the world go by, listening to the music that seemed to float in the air every summer night. When there were enough players, the boys would ride bikes down to Riverside Drive Park to play hardball. While in the outfield daydreaming I would always gaze at the Circle Line ferry sailing up the Hudson River, tracing the coast of Manhattan over and over again. Looking across the Hudson River, I would catch glimpses of the Palisades Amusement Park Roller Coaster.

Other times, we'd pedal our bikes over the Macombs Dam Bridge, which carried us over the Harlem River past the old Polo Grounds, where Willie Mays and the New York Giants played baseball. We only had a quarter of a mile left to go on our way to a Yankee Stadium game where "The Mick", Mickey Mantle was playing. Like countless other kids, we dreamed of catching a fly ball or a home run hit out of the park. A minor miracle we believed might happen if we were just in the right place at the right time. Harlem was a place that claimed you. It was impossible not to be shaped by it.

Life changed when my parents divorced. One day the phone rang, my mother answered and the voice on the other end was a bookie saying my father owed a large debt. My mother heard bodily harm would be next if the debt was not paid. My father had gotten over his head betting on the horses and Trotters. I was too young to understand all the reasons, but I felt the shift deeply. The family I knew became two separate worlds. Through it all, my mother remained our anchor, strong, steady, and determined to keep moving forward.

Around that time, New York City's school integration efforts began. I was bused from P.S. 186 to P.S. 86 in the Bronx, a predominantly Jewish school. Everything felt different. Hall monitors wore crisp white sashes with shiny badges. Boys came to school wearing bolo ties, a fashion unfamiliar to me. I wore a bow tie. Although I stood out, I carried myself with quiet pride. It was my first experience navigating a space where I was one of the few Black students, an early lesson in difference and belonging. I didn't know it then, but that experience would prepare me for future moments on Martha's Vineyard.

Eventually, my mother, sister, and I left my father and Harlem. We moved to Bedford-Stuyvesant, Brooklyn, to live with our Grandmother Pansy, at 103 Chauncey Street. This two-story brownstone marked another shift in my young life. My grandmother's home was different from our three-bedroom apartment in Harlem. Giant maple trees lined the Chauncey Street sidewalk. I will never forget the black wrought iron fence and the small square front yard, as well as the eight steps to climb before ringing the front doorbell. My grandmother rented the upstairs to a couple that were dear friends, and a studio to a very quiet, low-profile man whom we called Uncle Larry. He was a beatnik. Loved his jazz and would let me visit while he played his flute and listened to Xylophonist Cal Tjader, all the while burning his punk incense sticks. Sometimes, I would catch Uncle Larry jamming in the park across the street with other beatniks on Bongos, Conga drums, and flute. Brooklyn had a different energy, less hectic but no less alive. Children played until the sun dipped below the rooftops. My mother's words to me after dinner, when I asked to go back out to play, would always be, "Don't let the street lights catch you." That was her way of letting me know to be home before darkness sets. Same as my old block in Harlem, neighbors sat on stoops to talk about everything and nothing at all. It was a place of small joys and quiet discoveries. One of the neighborhood's points of pride was knowing that Jackie Gleason, one of television's biggest stars, lived on Chauncey Street. It made our block feel special having a celebrity live just down the street from us.

Across the street from our Brooklyn home was Fulton Street Park, where we played football on fall afternoons, where people walked their dogs. One day during a game of football, I was tackled hard, and my head landed squarely in a pile of dog shit. Everyone around me burst out in laughter as I jumped up, horrified, embarrassed, and smelling. I sprinted across the street to my grandmother Pansy's house to clean up. Looking back, that day always makes me laugh. It was one of those perfectly embarrassing childhood moments that sticks with you for life.

I attended P.S. 21, two blocks away, for one year. Spent many days running home after school because I was the new kid, and had to take a beating to belong. The thing is, I was never caught for my beating. I could outrun everyone.

Brooklyn taught me how to listen and observe. It was there that I began to understand my mother's strength and the bond I shared with my sister Vanessa. It was there that I started to dream beyond what I could see, even if I did not yet know what those dreams were.

Even as a child, I was curious about the world beyond the city blocks I knew so well. I would look down Chauncey Street and ask myself in wonder what lay past Brooklyn, past Harlem, past everything familiar. That curiosity would carry me far, across oceans and into a life I could never have imagined. It was more than a question; it was a calling.

*Home 501 West 143rd Street, Harlem, New York City*

*(L–R) Anthony Alleyne, Audrey Alleyne, Gladstone Alleyne. Vanessa Alleyne*

*Grandmother's Home, 103 Chauncey Street, Brooklyn, New York*

# II

# Part II

*Martha's Vineyard Years*

2

## Chapter 2

## Island Roots: Martha's Vineyard

*~ A peaceful haven offering many opportunities*

In the summer of 1962, my grandmother took my mother, sister Vanessa, and me on a vacation that would change our lives. After driving five hours, we boarded a ferry in Woods Hole, Massachusetts, heading to Martha's Vineyard. An island I heard people talk about in passing. When the ferry docked in Oak Bluffs, the air smelled of salt, and the sound of seagulls was ever-present. As cars and people exited the ferry, we witnessed young kids diving for coins, yelling, "How bout a Coin, how bout a Coin?" I watched with awe. Everything seemed to move more slowly.

We stayed with Emma Maitland, a striking, broad-shouldered

woman with a quiet demeanor, a voice that could fill a room, and a laugh that was only hers. Emma was a dancer at the Moulin Rouge in Paris and a boxer from 1920 to 1930, earning the World's Lightweight Female Boxing Championship. She owned a huge evergreen-colored two-story home with yellow-trimmed windows on Dukes County Road in Oak Bluff. She rented rooms each summer to Black families who came for rest and peace. My grandmother knew her from friends in New York. That summer, Emma's house was alive with the sounds of kids, the clatter of pots and pans in the kitchen, and the smell of porgies frying. Her backyard had the greenest grass and a small studio cottage with plenty of chairs and loungers. The grill was always smokin' with chicken and ribs, while conversations with drinks in hand were the norm.

The first night on the island, Vanessa and I slept on Emma's screened-in porch. It was the first time I had ever slept so close to nature. Through the screens, I could see fireflies blinking in the darkness. The air was cool and still, with the deafening sounds of crickets chirping and the distant sound of the ferry horn. It was both strange and comforting to be so far from the city's constant noise. I'll never forget my first night on MV because I could not go to sleep. The chirping sound of the crickets would keep me awake.

Most of the families who rented from Emma in the summer were African-American teachers, doctors, and professionals from Boston, New York, Philly, and Washington, DC. One man stood out because he didn't seem to fit the pattern. He was white, quiet, and comfortable in their company. His name was Phil. He helped Emma with repairs around the house and was always doing something with his hands, fixing a screen, tightening a hinge, hauling firewood. My mother, Audrey, noticed him too. Evenings on the screened-in porch, they would talk and laugh as the sky turned deep blue and the island settled into night.

For my mother, going to Martha's Vineyard was more than a summer escape; it was a leap of faith for all of us. What began as a vacation for African American families soon became the second-most influential island in my life. One afternoon, my mother took my sister and me to the beach in Oak Bluffs and told us she was going to remarry and that we would now have a stepfather. His name was Phil. The shocker, Phil, was the only white person I had ever seen hanging around and partying at Emma Maitland's home during our stays there. My sister and I knew nothing about this man. When our summer visit was over, we traveled up-island to the town of Chilmark, a small, quiet, rural place with three main roads: North Road, Middle Road, and South Road, also called State Road. Many heavily tree-lined dirt roads branched off the main roads. As a young city kid, they really scared me because the darkness made me feel the unknown. Traveling those roads took skill; when another car came from the opposite direction, someone had to pull over to let the other pass. It was all new to me, coming from Harlem.

Our new home was on South Road, a two-bedroom house that Phil built himself. Hardwood floors ran throughout, except in the kitchen and bathroom, which had green linoleum. My sister ended up getting the second bedroom about six months later when Phil designed a cubby-hole room for me. Complete with a closet, desk with built-in bookshelves, and a platform twin bed. Phil had two black miniature collies: Boots, the older, and Skippy, the younger. Phil was an industrious man, a carpenter by trade. He turned the attached two-car garage into a woodworking shop outfitted with a circular saw, band saw, lathe, a stand-up drill press, and hand tools I had never seen before. Sweet-smelling sawdust and neatly stacked lumber filled the space. I watched him build beautiful handmade pieces of furniture, coffee tables, chairs, and even his own scalloping boat. The fiberglassing process fascinated me; I had never seen anything like it.

Phil was also the Town Harbormaster for the fishing village of Menemsha, where boats tied up and weighed their catch, swordfish, cod, flounder, and lobster. He always brought seafood home: scallops, clams, flounder, cod, and lobster. We had so much lobster that my mother eventually stopped eating it. At Dutcher Dock in Menemsha, I learned to fish for squid bait. All I needed was a treble hook, white adhesive tape, a line, and a small lead weight. It was fun and challenging, especially trying not to get squirted with squid ink as I pulled in a catch. Squid ink does not come out of your clothes.

As a city kid, I never knew anything about lawn mowers, chain-saws for cutting winter cord wood, or brush cutters for clearing the yard. I was learning how to live on an island in New England. My first Christmas, I got a red truck bike with no gears, just one speed; to stop, you back-pedaled. My legs would get a serious workout going uphill. It was my country bike. I rode all over Chilmark, finding the best spots to pick blueberries in the summer. In the fall, I rode about five miles with a pail to pick bayberries. The aroma while picking was calming. The bayberries earned me pocket money.

Phil taught me a lot. He was strict in his own way. I realize now that he was so used to doing everything himself that having a young kid around required extra patience.

I was about to start sixth grade, my sister third, at the small two-room Menemsha School. My sister and I are the only Black students; everything was unfamiliar. The school had only seventeen students, grades 1–3 in one classroom and 4–6 in the other. My sixth-grade class consisted of three students: myself and two girls. The experience was nothing like what I imagined.

On November 22, 1963, when President John F. Kennedy was assassinated in Dallas, the two teachers met briefly, then decided school was over for the day, and sent everyone home early. That night, the silence was so complete it felt as if the whole world were holding its breath. Crickets filled the darkness with their chirping. The sounds of Chilmark were so different from the noise of the city I had always known. It was my second night when silence itself kept me awake.

Life on the island came with new challenges. Chilmark was an all-white town, and we were the only Blacks living there. My sister and I had to learn what it meant to grow up in a place where we were often seen as outsiders. But my mother, determined, fearless, and deeply involved in the fight for justice, made her presence known. In November 1963, just after President Kennedy's assassination, she became treasurer of the first NAACP chapter on Martha's Vineyard. She was a civil rights trailblazer, and her courage taught me that you don't wait for change, you help build it.

My mother was never a stay-at-home housewife; she always had a job. Living on Martha's Vineyard was new territory for all of us. One day, she answered a want-ad in the weekly island paper, the Vineyard Gazette, for a position at the island's only travel agency. I don't know what the hiring process was, but she got the job right away. We lived up-island in Chilmark, and the office was in Vineyard Haven on Main Street, about a twenty-minute drive. I remember her bringing home three massive catalogs labeled OAG Vol. 1-3. I later learned OAG stood for Official Airline Guide. My mother became known as the travel agent to see on Martha's Vineyard. Years later, she opened her own office, Dukes Travel Service, in Oak Bluffs.

Phil introduced me to calluses. In early spring 1964, he handed me a shovel and taught me how to turn soil for a garden in our backyard, a 20 × 30-foot plot. In April, the ground was still semi-hard from winter, and my skinny arms and legs struggled to push the spade deep enough. Phil worked one end while I wrestled with the other. By day's end, my hands were covered in blisters. Phil showed me his and said, "You'll be getting many more around here." What I didn't know was that the ground had to be turned two more times before we could plant. The last turnover involved spreading cow manure for fertilizer. This twelve-year-old from the city suddenly had a new life.

Planting was my first geometry lesson. Vegetables had to be spaced just right to maximize room for growth and allow multiple plantings each season. We started with small crops, radishes, and carrots, then moved on to tomatoes, cucumbers, potatoes, cantaloupe, corn, string beans, and watermelon. Watching the garden grow meant daily work: watering, weeding, and keeping pests at bay. Bugs, birds, rabbits, and deer were constant challenges.

When harvest time came, the reward was real. The next project was canning, a process new to all of us. From turning the soil in early April to sealing jars in late October, we learned how satisfying self-sufficiency could be. My favorite part was making jelly. From our garden, we produced jars of tomato jelly, something I never heard of and thought I would never enjoy until I tasted it. Then came grape jelly, and best of all, beach plum jelly, so good my mother rationed it to make it last. One other special recipe that my mother never disclosed was her well-known, tasty BBQ sauce. Many friends and family have tried to get me to give up the ingredients. Mom's secret sauce has remained a secret. I'm the sole keeper of her special lick-your-fingers BBQ sauce.

The island wasn't without surprises. One evening in November 1965, as we sat down to dinner, the lights in our house went out. The darkness was total, no streetlights, no distant glow. Phil brought out flashlights and candles, and for hours we listened to a battery-powered shortwave radio. We finally learned it was the Northeast Blackout of 1965. Power remained out for thirteen hours. It was frightening but unforgettable, a reminder of how connected we all are, even in a quiet corner of an island.

Despite the differences and adjustments, Martha's Vineyard became home. I learned to swim in its cold waters, explored its trails and beaches, and built friendships that would last a lifetime. The island taught me patience and observation, helping me notice the changing tides, the subtle shifts of the seasons, and the quiet strength that comes from stillness.

Martha's Vineyard was more than just a new address. It was the second island that shaped my life, a place that taught me who I was and prepared me for the journeys still to come.

*Emma Maitland & Grandmother Pansy*

*Menemsha School, Chilmark, Massachusetts*

*My Mother, Audrey, Owner of Dukes Travel Service – The Island's Gateway to the World*

# 3

## Chapter 3

## Coming of Age on Martha's Vineyard

*~ Teenage years on a country island*

By the time I reached high school, Martha's Vineyard was no longer just a new place; it was home. The island had become the backdrop of my teenage years. It was where I learned who I was, tested my limits, and began to imagine the life that lay ahead of me.

School life was different here; high school was in Oak Bluffs. It was there that I began to see more of the world beyond Chilmark. My classmates came from other towns, backgrounds, and experiences. I was learning not just from books like Manchild in the Promised Land by Claude Brown, and The Spook Who Sat By the Door by Sam Greelee, but from people by the way they spoke, how they saw the world, and how they treated each other. These lessons would stay with me far beyond those school days.

Martha's Vineyard Regional High School was a new world for me. Between 1967 and 1970, I was fortunate to have someone who became both my coach and lifelong mentor, Coach Jay Schofield. He taught me how to make strides not only in sports, but in life. He possessed a keen ability to spot and develop an athlete's talent. As a coach and teacher, he made sure student understood that sports were a stepping stone to life.

The most impactful advice he gave me upon graduation was: "If there is something you want to do in life, don't hesitate and lose that opportunity, go for it!" Those words have guided me through many of the decisions I've made throughout my life.

In high school, being on a sports team was a big deal. I ran cross-country in the fall, basketball in the winter, and track and field in the spring. In my freshman year, I tried out for the football team because I could run. During the first practice, on my very first run, I was tackled hard. Being the skinny kid, I peeled myself off the ground and realized this was not for me. Later that afternoon, as I was leaving the locker room, I approached Coach Schofield, who coached cross-country, and asked if I could try out for his team. The rest is history.

In my sophomore year, I was the fastest runner on the team. Coach gave me a solid purple jersey and told the team to stay as close to me as possible during cross-country meets. During my remaining three years at Martha's Vineyard High, I was the fastest runner in the school. In track, I held the 880-yard record for more than twenty years. Looking back, it's interesting how those early days outrunning the boys in Brooklyn helped develop my endurance as a runner. Who knew?

In the 1960s, it was a big deal to wear a varsity school jacket in the school's colors, purple and white. What set you apart was earning the big purple "V" and having it sewn on. The most prestigious of all was earning a gold bar, which signified another year on the team. By the time I graduated, I had earned three "V"s and three gold bars for each of the following: cross-country, basketball, and track and field. Only one purple "V" was allowed on your jacket, but it represented all the hard work behind it. The "V" stood for Vineyarders.

June 1970 arrived, and it was time for graduation. To my surprise, Coach was working on a cross-country scholarship for me at Quinnipiac College. But another reality was weighing heavily on me, the Vietnam War. The draft was on everyone's mind. Every evening, Walter Cronkite reported on CBS News the number of U.S. military casualties and tonnage of napalm bombs dropped. The thought of being drafted loomed large. College offered no shield if your draft number was called. I had a decision to make. I spoke to my mother and asked if she would sign the paperwork to allow me to enlist in the military. She replied, "Yes, if that's what you want to do."

Two months before graduation, all the military recruiters were scheduled to visit the high school to interview interested students. The Air Force was my first choice, but that recruiter did not make the trip. My second choice was the Navy. I spoke with the Navy recruiter, who scheduled my entrance testing exam in New Bedford. I passed the exam and my mother signed the enlistment papers. I was seventeen years old. On Thursday, June 11, 1970, just five days after graduation, I was sworn in. "I'm in the Navy now."

Years later, when I returned to Martha's Vineyard after my Navy career, I discovered that Walter Cronkite, one of America's most respected journalists, had retired to Chilmark, not far from where we once lived.  It made me smile to think that as I was growing up, dreaming of the world beyond the island, he, too, was looking out at the same fields and waters. It reminded me how small the world really is, and how the places that shape us often shape others, too.

The island shaped my teenage years in countless ways. I gained responsibility by helping around the house, found joy in riding my bike along long stretches of country roads, and hitchhiked around the island, exploring beaches and trails that seemed to stretch on forever. Even the quiet taught me something: how to listen, how to reflect, and how to appreciate the stillness that city life rarely allows. The island had prepared me for life at sea; I just didn't know how soon I'd be surrounded by water again.

*Entering Chilmark on State / South Road*

## CROSS COUNTRY

*1972 Martha's Vineyard Regional High School Cross Country Team*

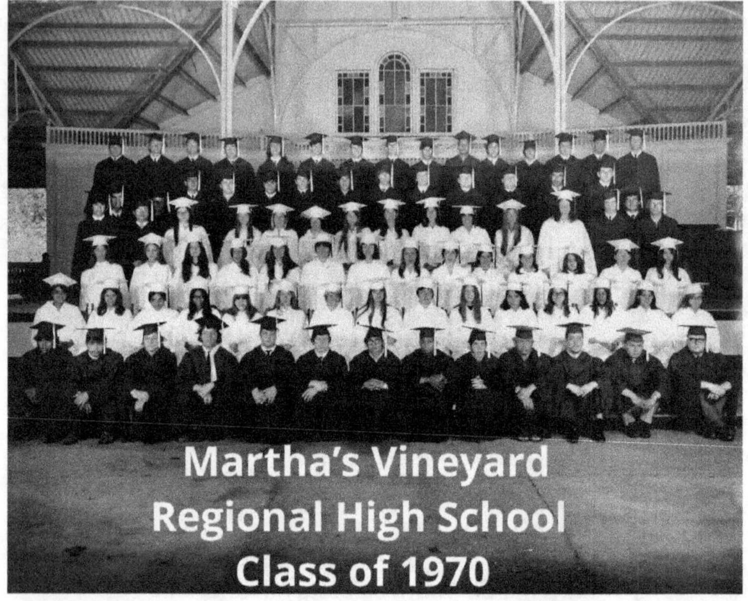


*Class of 1970 Graduation Photo*

# III

# Part III

*Life in Uniform*

# 4

# Chapter 4

## A New Direction: Joining the Navy

*~ Haze gray and underway*

As my teenage years on Martha's Vineyard came to an end, I found myself standing at a crossroads. The island that had once felt so big and full of discovery now felt small. I was restless, eager to see more of the world beyond the ferry docks. Like so many young men of my generation, I was looking for purpose and realized I wouldn't find it by standing still. With world events and the Vietnam War unfolding, I made a decision that would change the course of my life: I joined the United States Navy.

Leaving Martha's Vineyard was bittersweet. I was leaving behind everything familiar, the woods and beaches, the people who had watched me grow, and the island rhythms that had shaped me. But I also felt a pull I couldn't ignore. I wanted to challenge myself, prove myself, and be part of something larger than my small world. The Navy promised all of that and more: discipline, direction, and a chance to see beyond the horizon that had always called to me.

My last ferry ride from the island felt different. The unknown was ahead. That night, I would be sleeping in a totally different environment. Many thoughts raced through my head as the ferry sailed away. This would be a long day of unknowns. I was on my way to be sworn into the U.S. Navy.

Once off the ferry, I caught the bus to the Selective Service Complex in Providence, Rhode Island. The center was a two-story building with offices, exam rooms, and a large induction hall. About a hundred guys from all over New England were about to be sworn into all branches of the military. Some were draftees, some enlisted, and others were court-ordered to join. The process was foreign to me, but I followed every instruction.

Upon entering, everyone was ordered to sit and wait for their name to be called. When mine was called, I entered an office, filled out forms, and was given my service number, my identification. It's a number every military member will never forget. Then came a quick physical exam, and I returned to the big room until everyone was processed. Some were rejected for various reasons and didn't complete the process.

Next, we were instructed to enter the large induction room decorated with military flags and the American flag in the center.

An officer stood before us, his voice booming as if the world had personally offended him. Some inductees smirked; others looked uneasy. As for me, I just listened, observed, and followed instructions. About 75 of us passed and were sworn in as Army, Air Force, Navy, and Marine Corps members, heading to boot camp. With the oath complete, I was bused to the Providence airport for a flight to Chicago's O'Hare.

## Boot Camp – Great Lakes, Illinois

Navy boot camp at Great Lakes, Illinois, was a shock to my world. The easy pace of island life was replaced by barking orders and days that began before dawn. I learned quickly that the Navy wasn't just about ships and uniforms; it was about teamwork, discipline, and resilience. Every day tested me, from physical endurance to mental toughness, but each test made me stronger. Slowly, I began to understand that I was becoming part of something bigger than myself.

Upon arrival, about fifty guys from all over the country were grouped as Company 217. It was unlike anything I'd ever experienced: guys from rural Texas, the cities of Chicago and Washington D.C., the coasts of California, and the bayous of Louisiana, all walks of life together. We spent our first night in boot camp's indoctrination section, Camp Barry. It was "O-dark-thirty" when a tall First-Class Petty Officer in summer tropical whites entered the barracks. He was our Company Commander (CC). I remember his opening words: "Get out of those racks, Boots!" This was our first official morning in the Navy. "You are not recruits until we leave Camp Barry's indoctrination," he barked. "For the next ten days, you will be called Boots. From now on, you no longer live in your mama's house. In boot camp, you live in a barracks. That's your first ship. You don't sleep in beds, you sleep in racks. You don't walk on floors, you walk on decks. There are no walls, only bulkheads. Ships don't have doors; they have hatches. You don't drink from water fountains; they're scuttle-butts. The Navy doesn't have bathrooms; they're called heads." All this was thrown at us before dawn, before breakfast in the mess hall. It was our CC's job to teach Company 217 how to live like sailors, turning fifty civilians into Navy men ready for the fleet.

During indoctrination, all "boots" wore blue ball caps. Camp Barry was also where every boot received dog tags, their name, service number, religion, and blood type stamped on aluminum. The dull clinking sound of those tags never left my ears. They were a constant reminder of identity and mortality. We were then issued uniforms: dungarees, chambray shirts, underwear, dress and undress blues, summer whites, raincoat, pea-coat, boots, shoes, and socks, all to be hemmed by civilian workers. Next came lessons in how to wash, fold, and stow them "the Navy way." I remember wondering if a magician could really fit that many uniforms into the tiny locker space we were given.

After completing indoctrination, Company 217 marched proudly to our new barracks at Camp Dewey. Wearing our White Dixie cup, for the first time, feeling like a sailor, though still in boot camp. The first thing noticeable about our new barracks was the smell of "Brasso", the Navy's metal polish. Now the real work began, twelve weeks of marching, drilling, inspections, and instruction that would shape us into sailors.

## Training and Tradition

In boot camp, we marched everywhere in formation to breakfast, lunch, dinner, classes, and drills. Our first class at Camp Dewey took place in one of the many training buildings. Before entering, every recruit removed his cover (the White Dixie cup) and held it in his right hand. Once inside, we stood at our desks until the instructor arrived. Our first instructor wrote his rank and name on the board, then said, "You're each being issued the Navy Sailor's Bible. This is **The Bluejacket's Manual**, over 700 pages of naval history, protocol, and seamanship. It was our guide to everything about Navy life.

The company's first drill session was in July, on the hot tarmac, where we were issued M14 rifles, nine pounds each, inert for training. They were ours for the duration of boot camp. Two men were exceptions: the Recruit Company Petty Officer (RCPO), the company leader, who carried a sheath and sword, and the Guide-on, who held an aluminum flag pole with the blue company flag marked 217 in white numerals. I was selected as the Guide-on. The Drill Instructor made his choices based on observation and performance during Camp Barry. Drilling in the sun was grueling, but our company began to move as one, fifty individuals becoming a single team.

## Becoming a Sailor

It was during this time that I began to see the Navy not just as a job, but as a calling. The life lessons I learned on Martha's Vineyard, patience, observation, and adaptability, were now the skills I leaned on every day. Whether mastering drills, following orders, or pushing myself beyond what I thought were my limits, I was laying the foundation for a career that would span decades.

I still remember the day I graduated from boot camp. Standing in formation in my Navy Dress Whites, I felt a pride unlike anything I'd known. It wasn't just about completing training; it was about taking the first step into a new life. The boy from Harlem, who had grown up surrounded by water on an island, now belonged to a Navy that sailed every sea on Earth. My world had just become a whole lot bigger.

As I prepared for my first assignment, I knew I was setting out on a journey that would take me places I had only dreamed of. There would be challenges ahead, but also opportunities I couldn't yet imagine. Joining the Navy wasn't just a decision. It was the moment my life's direction shifted forever. My first assignment would take me from the classroom to the fleet; my education was just beginning.

*(BJM) Navy Sailor's Bible*

5

# Chapter 5

Life in Uniform

~ You're in the Navy now

I was barely out of my teens when I raised my right hand and took the Military Oath of Enlistment into the United States Navy. It was September 1970, fresh out of Boot Camp with my first set of orders in hand. I was assigned to the USS *Little Rock* (CLG-4), home-ported in Newport, Rhode Island. The ship had just returned from serving as the U.S. Sixth Fleet Flagship in Gaeta, Italy (1967–1970).

The Little Rock, a Light Cruiser, felt like a floating city. I was both excited and nervous as I stepped aboard the first time. She carried Talos missiles, the largest surface-launched anti-air and surface-defense weapons of the time. Her crew complement was over 1,100: 940 enlisted, 43 officers, and 150 Marines. Steel passageways echoed with boots, machinery, and the hum of shipboard life. The air smelled faintly of oil and salt, and the fluorescent-lit passageways stretched endlessly in every direction. It was a new world, and I was determined to make something of myself in it.

Assigned to the Third Division, my job was to swab decks and paint the ship's aft section, both interior and exterior. Deck division sailors also stood deck watches in port and at sea. Thinking back to Boot Camp and the Bluejacket's Manual, I remembered: standing the watch is the most crucial duty in the Navy.

The Little Rock was an old ship; she had been around since the 1940s, and unlike most, her quarterdeck was laid in teak wood, not steel. Maintaining that deck's shine and preserving its grain was the pride of the deck divisions: the Boatswain's Mates, Seamen, and Apprentices. I was new aboard, an E-2 Seaman Apprentice (SA). Every morning at 0500, we were on deck, wetting down and holy-stoning the teak. I quickly told myself, This is not for me. The berthing compartment where we slept was cramped, loud, and filled with a smell only sailors could tolerate. I had to adjust and adapt. The best comparison I can offer is the old World War II movie Destination Tokyo; that's what shipboard life was like.

Early on, I noticed something else, something more profound. This was 1970, during the Civil Rights Era, and I couldn't help but notice that most of the deck divisions were comprised of Black sailors. Cooks in the galley were primarily Black and Filipino.

The supply division looked the same. I told myself: That will not be me for four years.

## Dry Dock and Hard Lessons

After returning from overseas, the Little Rock was scheduled for a significant overhaul in the Boston Naval Shipyard. The six-month dry dock period exposed us to the coldest winter I'd ever experienced. There was no heat aboard the ship; we slept and ate on nearby barges. The silver lining was modernization. Berthing racks were upgraded from canvas to coffin-locker style bunks, a luxury compared to the old ones.

Once the overhaul was complete, Little Rock emerged rejuvenated. Still an aging cruiser. We began workups, months of sea trials, and inspections in the Caribbean and Guantanamo Bay to prepare for deployment. There were drills of every kind: General Quarters, Fire, and Man Overboard. After passing inspection, the crew finally understood what Boot Camp had been preparing us for: the precision and readiness demanded at sea.

## A Chance to Advance

After a year aboard, I had the opportunity to apply for a rating, a Navy occupation. Up to that point, I'd been a non-designated Seaman, doing whatever deck work was assigned. I told myself, I will not spend my Navy career just painting and scrubbing.

An opportunity became available in the form of a Striker Board, an interview panel for young sailors seeking technical ratings. The board consisted of five Chief Petty Officers and one officer. I reported to the Chiefs' Mess in Dress Blues, nervous, palms sweating, unsure what to expect from men who had 12 years or more of service; most were Vietnam veterans.

They began with fundamental questions about shipboard life. One Chief asked, "Would you be interested in being a Postal Clerk in the ship's post office?" I answered honestly: "I'm looking for a job where I can learn, grow, and make the Navy a career." That surprised the Board. An 18-year-old Black E-2 Seaman Apprentice saying he wanted to stay in for 20 years got their attention. Another Chief asked if I knew anything about photography. I replied, "No, but I think it would be an interesting job to learn, and one I could build a future with." The interview ended.

A week later, I was transferred to X Division, in the Operations Department home to Personnelmen (PN), Yeomen (YN), Drafts-men (DM), and Photographer's Mates (PH). Packing my sea-bag and leaving the deck division was one of my proudest moments. Some of the brothers laughed and said I'd be back in a week. They were wrong. Soon, I was learning how to shoot, process, and print black-and-white photos. The ship's lone Photographer's Mate (PH2), an experienced photographer, was preparing to separate from the Navy. I started small, shooting re-enlistment ceremonies, handshakes, and cake cuttings, learning to see through the camera's lens. Then came the mistake that changed my life.

### The Chemical Mix-Up

One evening, the PH2 was photographing the Captain's 25th wedding anniversary aboard the ship.  While he was at the party, I was in the lab mixing fresh photographic chemicals. When he returned and began developing the film, thirty seconds in, he shouted, "What the FUCKKK!" I mixed the chemicals in the wrong bottles, fixer where developer should be.  The entire event's negatives were ruined. It was the kind of error that could have ended my Navy career before it began.  But Captain Cullins, the Commanding Officer, saw something in me I hadn't yet seen in myself. Instead of punishment, he secured approval for me to attend the U.S. Naval Schools of Photography in Pensacola, Florida, on Temporary Additional Duty (TAD). It was the opportunity that changed my life.

### Learning the Craft

Two months later, I reported to Building 1500, U.S. Naval Schools of Photography, Pensacola, Florida, for PH "A" school. The basement was lined with darkrooms, the first deck with offices, classrooms, and the second with advanced photography courses. Every Navy Photographer knows Building 1500, and the smell of fixer that permeates every corner.

For twelve weeks, I had hands-on experience learning different cameras, lighting, composition, and photographic equations such as hyperfocal distance. I learned how to document naval operations, record history, and capture the images that informed decisions at the highest levels.

While attending photo school, I was surprised to run into three other brothers. In the barracks, we quickly found each other's room and established a fast bond. We were shocked that four brothers were at PH "A" school at the same time. We would spend weekends together buying and drinking Boone's Farm Strawberry Hill Wine or Ripple Pagan Pink from the base package store. While hanging out, we solidified our oneness by creating our own DAP handshake. We were cool! Four Navy brothers at the U.S. Naval Schools of Photography together.

I graduated from the U.S. Naval Schools of Photography. I was no longer an untrained sailor, now a Photographer's Mate Airman (PHAN), officially rated. After a short leave period, I rejoined the Little Rock in Athens, Greece, where the ship was deployed. The Navy-wide advancement results had just arrived, and to my surprise, I was promoted to PH3. It was validation and the beginning of my career behind the lens. I celebrated my promotion on liberty by photographing the sights of Athens, Greece, including the Acropolis and the Parthenon. The perfect way to mark a new chapter.

## Social Tension at Sea

The early '70s were turbulent years. The Vietnam War still raged, and race relations throughout America and the Navy were strained. By the time I returned to the Little Rock, now serving again as Sixth Fleet Flagship, racial inequality aboard ship mirrored what was happening in the states. Black sailors were frustrated by limited advancement and inconsistent enforcement of regulations. Admiral Elmo Zumwalt, Chief of Naval

Operations, recognized the growing tension and began implementing reforms.  Despite being undermanned, 800 sailors instead of 915, morale was low.  Drug use was an issue, and tempers sometimes flared.  One night on the mess decks, an argument between a Black sailor and a white sailor over alcohol turned violent. The fight was broken up, but later reignited in a berthing compartment when the white sailor retaliated with a dogging wrench, a heavy steel tool used for securing hatches. Chaos spread quickly through the berthing compartment.  By 2215, it had become a race riot; 20 to 25 Black sailors went after white sailors with dogging wrenches and flashlights, as they slept. The Commanding Officer and Executive Officer responded immediately, calling all officers and Chiefs to their messes to stabilize the ship. The situation calmed by 0330. Several sailors sustained injuries; one white sailor, one Black sailor, and one Black Marine were later sent to Naples, Italy, for court-martial. Three months later, I re-enlisted in Gaeta, determined to keep moving forward.

*Pax River*

My next set of orders took me ashore to the Naval Air Test Center, Patuxent River, Maryland. It was 1974, and I had just gotten married before reporting for duty. The base's Photo Lab was huge, with 25 Photographer's Mates, and three civilian technicians. Walking in for the first time, I was overwhelmed by the sight of multiple darkrooms, a full portrait studio, and five Kodak aerial film processors the size of small vans. These machines developed 5- and 10-inch-wide aerial film in 200, 300, and 500-foot lengths. The smell of chemicals filled the air, familiar and strangely comforting.

Pax River was the heart of Naval Aviation. The sky thundered daily with F-4 Phantoms, F-14 Tomcats, and classified C-130 flights. Our lab documented everything from new system tests to crash investigations. Pax River was also where I saw the weight of the job. I documented aircraft mishaps and the aftermath of suicides, images that demanded respect and composure. Each assignment deepened my understanding of service, sacrifice, and the human cost of military life.

In 1975, I photographed one of the most personal moments of my life, the birth of my daughter. Standing behind the lens in that delivery room remains one of my proudest moments.

Once again, I returned to Pensacola for a two-week course in Color Photography to advance my technical skills. By the end of my third year of shore duty, my advancement exam came in, and my next promotion to PH2 was official.

When the time came to choose my next assignment, I wanted to stay the course. I raised my hand once again, took the Oath of Re-enlistment, and prepared for my next tour of sea duty, aboard the USS *Dwight D. Eisenhower* (CVN-69), under construction.

Through it all, I continued to grow as a photographer, sailor, and leader. From the mistake that nearly ended my career on the Little Rock, to the trust of Captain Cullins, to the honor of my promotions and the work at Pax River, these early years in uniform laid the foundation for everything that followed. The Navy taught me that growth often begins where comfort ends, that leadership sometimes looks like a second chance, and that the power of an image can extend far beyond the frame. Most of all, I learned that the Navy was exactly where I was meant to be.

As I prepared to step aboard the nuclear-powered aircraft carrier, USS *Dwight D. Eisenhower* (CVN-69), I felt the weight of experience behind me and new horizons ahead. I was no longer the young seaman who once swabbed decks on the Little Rock. I was now a Photographer's Mate Second Class, ready for the challenge of documenting life at sea aboard one of the Navy's most powerful warships.

*USS Little Rock (CLG-4) Sixth Fleet Flag Ship*

*U.S. Naval Schools of Photography, Bldg. 1500, Pensacola, Florida*

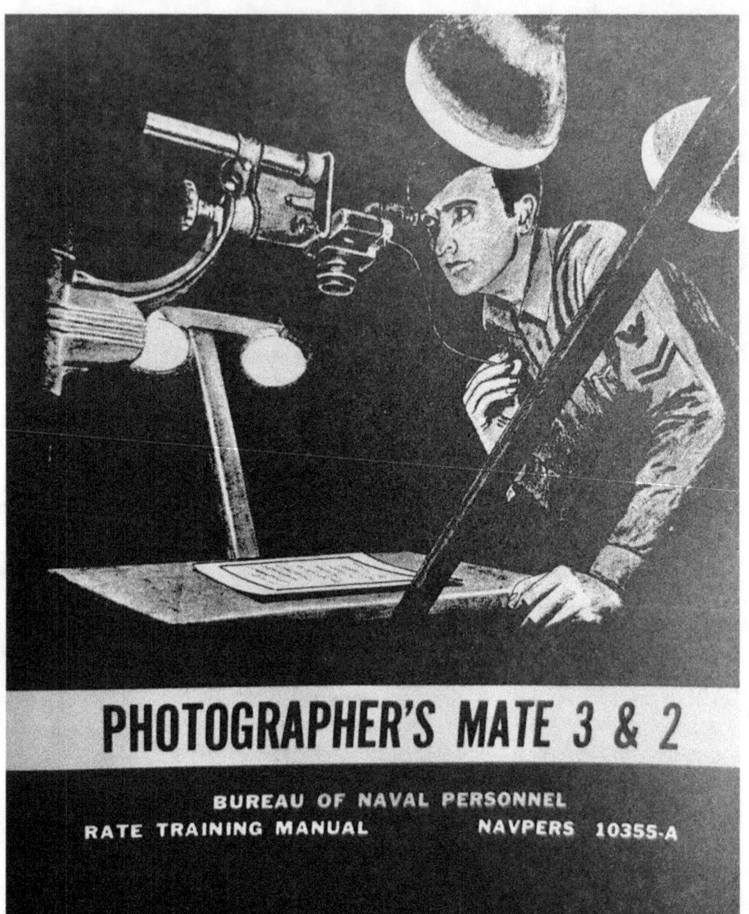


*Photographer's Mate 3 &2 Training Manual*

# 6

# Chapter 6

## USS Dwight D. Eisenhower (CVN-69) – 1st Tour

*~ I LIKE IKE*

In July 1977, I reported for duty aboard the nuclear-powered aircraft carrier USS *Dwight D. Eisenhower* (CVN-69). Construction completion was about two months away. This ship was massive, more than three football fields in length, capable of carrying over 90 aircraft, and destined to be home to more than 5,000 men at sea.  Right away, everyone knew Eisenhower's nickname, IKE, as the ship was fondly called. Newly reporting personnel joined while the ship was still under construction; these sailors formed the pre-commissioning crew, known as Plank-Owners, the original crew who would bring the ship to life when she was commissioned.

IKE was unique. The energy aboard was electric. We were writing the first chapter of this nuclear-powered carrier's history, and I was part of a small group of photographers tasked with building the photo lab and documenting every stage from the keel up.  One such memory occurred when IKE was in dry dock. I photographed the ship's four massive, shining bronze propellers, each 25 feet in diameter, weighing 66,000 pounds. Standing under the Eisenhower, looking up at the mammoth size of the ship and propellers, was an opportunity that few Navy photographers would experience. The ship's motto said it all: "I LIKE IKE."

## Life Aboard the New Giant

The ship was a floating city, the largest vessel in the Navy. Coming from shore duty at Pax River, the scale of carrier life was unimaginable: thousands of sailors, constant motion, and a tempo that never slowed. Flight operations roared above us, and every day brought new opportunities to capture a moment of the Navy in action.

From the start, I was impressed by our photo division. We had systems for film handling, processing workflows, equipment maintenance (PMS), and photo aerial readiness. IKE's photo division operated two separate labs: the main lab, two decks below the hangar bay, and a second lab inside the ship's intelligence center on the O3 level just below the flight deck. We trained hard and shot harder.  Providing Naval Investigative Service (NIS) photographic services, documenting everything from flight-deck operations to replenishment at sea, and processing miles of aerial film to capturing the rhythm of daily life aboard the Navy's newest nuclear aircraft carrier.

## Aerial Missions and Catapult Launches

It was aerial photography that lit something inside me. I qualified to fly helicopter photo missions, and later, for one of the rarest experiences of my career: catapult launches off the flight deck in an A-6 refueling tanker and an S-3 Viking. To prepare, I trained in the Martin-Baker ejection seat, learned emergency procedures, and completed a grueling survival-swim qualification that pushed me far beyond my comfort zone. It was tough, but worth every exhausting minute in the pool and ocean. The day of that flight remains unforgettable. I suited up in flight gear, stepped onto the deck, climbed into the navigator's seat, and strapped in beside the pilot. I checked my G-suit, oxygen connection, and camera one last time. As the engines roared and the catapult tension built, then *slam!*, we were hurled from zero to flying speed in under three seconds, flung off the deck into the open sky. Below us, the carrier shrank against the Atlantic. Through my lens, I captured IKE slicing through the sea, her deck alive with motion, a moving city projecting Naval power across the ocean. Later, the pilot connected with an Air Force KC-130 tanker for in-flight refueling training. With my camera tightly pressed against my oxygen mask, I photographed the precise moment our refueling probe met the tanker's hose at 15,000 feet. It was breathtaking to witness a combination of power, precision, and grace. Those frames would later appear in Navy publications and briefings, but for me, they were deeply personal proof of how far I had come since those early days mixing chemicals on the Little Rock.

## The Rhythm of the Sea

Life aboard the IKE followed the relentless rhythm of the ocean. Days blurred into nights, and nights into days, with flight ops dictating everything. We photographed carrier qualifications, drills, replenishments, award ceremonies, and the countless human moments that turned steel and systems into a community.

Our berthing compartment (3-64-1-L) was OP Division's world, forward on the third deck, packed with thirty-five photographers. During continuous flight ops, the noise never stopped: the thunder of catapults, the jolt of arrested landings, the deep hum of aircraft elevators. At first, sleeping through it was impossible. But I soon remembered New York City's constant pulse, and that memory taught me how to tune out chaos. Eventually, I could sleep soundly until the clang of the ship's bells or the sharp call of "General Quarters, General Quarters! All hands man your battle stations!" snapped us awake again.

## Ports of Call and World Horizons

We also saw the world. Ports of call became windows into history. Palma de Mallorca, Spain, is a city with its narrow streets and centuries-old stone buildings. Istanbul, Turkey, where the call to prayer echoed across the Bosporus. Athens, Greece, where I photographed from a third-story window of the USO, the county's Independence Day parade. Each port reminded me how vast the world truly is and how the Navy connected it.

## The 254-Day Deployment

In April 1980, President Jimmy Carter ordered *IKE* to the Indian Ocean in response to the Iran Hostage Crisis. We were to relieve the *USS Nimitz (CVN-68)*. The memory of photographing *IKE* pulling away from Pier 12 in Norfolk, Virginia, with families and girlfriends crying and waving goodbye. This really hit hard because no one knew how long we would be gone for this deployment. We remained at sea for 254 days, the longest deployment since World War II. It was a long and arduous deployment. To keep morale up, Captain James Mauldin authorized "Flight Deck Olympics" and "Steel Beach Cookouts". Secretary of the Navy Edward Hidalgo authorized a two-beer ration per man after 45 days or more at sea, subject to the ship Captain's approval. IKE had three separate "Beer Days", which dubbed the deployment as "The Six Pack Cruise". In July, IKE was granted an unscheduled five-day liberty port visit in Singapore. IKE's crew earned the Navy Unit Commendation Ribbon and the Navy-Marine Corps Expeditionary Medal for this extended period. Eight and a half months that tested every ounce of our strength and patience.

## A Plank-Owner's Pride

My advancement to PH1 wasn't just a promotion; it was validation. It represented a journey from a young sailor learning film exposure and camera composition on the Little Rock, to a seasoned photographer trusted to capture the Navy's story aboard the latest nuclear-powered aircraft carrier.  IKE was more than another assignment; it was a proving ground. A place where I tested myself, discovered my limits, and began to see a larger path ahead. I didn't know it yet, but my connection to Eisenhower wasn't over. This Plank-Owner would return.

My next set of orders would take me ashore once again, to Atlantic Fleet Audiovisual Command (AFAVC) in Norfolk, Virginia, a hub of innovation and visual communication for the Fleet. What awaited there would expand my lens even further, and eventually send me overseas to document a historic world event unfolding in real time.

*USS Dwight D. Eisenhower (CVN–69) with Two Gold Anchors*

*I LIKE IKE Pin*

*IKE Photo–Lab Plank Owner Patch*

7

# Chapter 7

## Atlantic Fleet Audiovisual Command / Naval Air Station Sigonella, Sicily

*~ Shore Duty & Sea Duty*

After almost four unforgettable years aboard the IKE, I left the flight deck behind and reported to Atlantic Fleet Audiovisual Command (AFAVC) in Norfolk, Virginia. It was 1980, and I arrived as a newly advanced Photographer's Mate First Class (PH1), ready to take everything I'd learned at sea and apply it ashore. The transition from carrier life to shore duty was dramatic. Gone were the rolling decks and catapults; in their place were offices, studios, and an ever-shifting schedule of projects that could range from shooting fleet-wide exercises and ships commissioning to recording weekly Navy News This Week video segments.

60

AFAVC's mission was as broad as the fleet itself. We supported commands across the Atlantic and Mediterranean, documenting operations, producing training materials, and providing visual coverage that shaped decisions and preserved history. No two days were the same. One week, we might be shooting an admiral's change of command; the next, we'd be on the pier capturing the return of a ship from deployment. The work required versatility, attention to detail, and a steady hand, qualities I had honed on the IKE.

Leadership became a bigger part of my life here. As one of the senior enlisted photographers, I was responsible not only for my own work but also for ensuring the performance of junior photographers. Instructing them on how to think ahead, anticipate the story, and prepare for the unexpected, entrusting them with the fundamentals of composition, exposure, and timing, while emphasizing the intangibles, how to stay calm when a mission shifted midstream, and how to earn trust through reliability and professionalism. Wanting them to succeed not just as photographers but as sailors who understood the weight of the story they were telling.

Audio Visual Command taught me the importance of logistics. Our jobs often came together unexpectedly, and we had to be ready to move at a moment's notice. I became meticulous about gear prep, checklists, and load-outs. Every Halliburton case was packed in order of use; every piece of equipment was double-checked before we stepped out the door. A successful shoot didn't just depend on skill behind the lens; it depended on preparation before the shutter ever clicked.

I recall one particular video assignment for Navy News This Week, an interview with Navy Master Chief Diver Carl Brashear, the first Black Navy Master Diver. This interview focused on his return to active duty after a diving accident in which he lost part of his lower left leg and had to prove to the Navy that he could still dive and serve his country. After the interview, Master Chief Brashear and I had the opportunity to discuss our respective careers as Black sailors. This conversation was deeply profound because we both knew the measures of performance required to prove ourselves and our abilities during a time of significant racial discrimination in the Navy. He then shared that Hollywood had approached him about shooting a movie documenting his Navy career. The film Men of Honor was released 17 years later, in November 2000, starring Cuba Gooding Jr. as Master Chief Diver Carl Brashear.

Norfolk, Virginia, was the home of Navy Combat Photographers, Combat Camera Group (CCG) for the Atlantic Fleet. The command consisted of two components: shore duty and sea duty. Combat Camera Photographers are trained in parachute jumping, underwater photography, and weapons training while keeping up with the latest photographic technology and equipment. For me to become a qualified Combat Camera Photographer Crew Chief meant returning to the U.S. Naval Schools of Photography in Pensacola, Florida, for six weeks. This was "B" School. A curriculum that covered motion picture recording, editing, sound recording, and additional training in video and studio production. After completing the course, I returned to Norfolk, Virginia.

Next came the assignment that would define my time at AFAVC:

a six-month sea-duty, Temporary Additional Duty (TAD) deployment to Naval Air Station Sigonella, located on the Italian
island of Sicily. I was to serve as Combat Camera Crew Chief,
leading a Combat Camera headquarters responsible for documenting fleet operations and contingency missions across
the Mediterranean. It was a significant responsibility, and an
opportunity I embraced fully.

Sigonella was a world apart from Norfolk. There were two
separate bases, NAS 1, NAS 2. NAS 1 was perched beneath the
looming presence of Mount Etna, its volcanic slopes visible from
almost every vantage point. The air smelled faintly of citrus, and
there I tasted my first blood orange, a small detail that somehow
captured the essence of Sicily itself. Life on base alternated
between intense bursts of activity and long stretches of quiet
preparation. The base photo lab became the nerve center for
everything, part workshop, part command post, part home. At
the end of the workday, base personnel took a fifteen-minute
bus ride to NAS 2. Our off-duty haven consisted of barracks, a
club, a gym, a swimming pool, a commissary, a mess hall, and
base housing for families.

Our most significant mission came in August 1982. We received
orders to deploy for the evacuation of Yasser Arafat and the
Palestine Liberation Organization (PLO) from Beirut, Lebanon,
in coordination with the 32nd Marine Amphibious Unit (32nd
MAU). The situation was tense and volatile. Beirut was a city
still bearing the scars of war. We set up operations with Marines
in a bombed-out warehouse riddled with bullets and blown out
windows in the port area. The mission required precision, discipline, and discretion. Our role was to document the evacuation

of Arafat and the PLO out of Beirut. The images would tell the story and serve as part of the historical record, photographing Marines maintaining order on the ground, civilians boarding ships under guarded watch, and the coordinated movements of U.S. and multinational forces offshore. Every frame mattered. We worked close to the action, often under uncertain conditions. These weren't just photographs; they captured history in the making. This Beirut assignment lasted two weeks.

Back at Sigonella, we spent long hours under the yellow glow of darkroom safe lights, processing and cataloging the images that told the story of that mission. Video was immediately flown back to Atlantic Fleet Audio Visual Command (AFAVC) headquarters in Norfolk, Virginia. The weight of it was not lost on us. We weren't just observers; we were participants in an operation that carried global implications. The work was intense, but it felt deeply meaningful.

There were lighter moments, too, trips to Catania, Palermo, and Agrigento that revealed the island of Sicily's warmth and history. Wandering through ancient ruins and vibrant markets reminded me of the privilege of serving in places most people only read about. Those moments offered balance and a reminder that even in a career defined by mission and duty, there was space for reflection and wonder.

By the time I rotated back to Norfolk, I carried more than exposed rolls of film. I brought back lessons in leadership, adaptability, and the power of imagery to shape how history is understood. AFAVC and Sigonella had stretched me in new ways. They taught me how to lead under pressure, plan for the unpredictable, and use a camera not just to record events but to reveal their deeper meaning.

The experience gained through Combat Camera Group and AFAVC prepared me for advancement. Soon, I would find myself wearing new anchors on my collar and leading from a different perspective. But before that, there was one more ship waiting for me, and a new level of leadership I was ready to embrace.

*Combat Camera Group Challenge Coin*

*Combat Camera Group Logo*

# 8

# Chapter 8

## USS Saipan (LHA-2) / Fleet Intelligence Center Europe and Atlantic

*~ Photo Intelligence Operations*

In 1983, a new phase of sea duty was my next assignment. A flight deck and well deck of the *USS Saipan (LHA-2)*. The Saipan, an amphibious assault ship, was a much different environment from the nuclear carrier I'd left. Where Eisenhower was vast and bustling, Saipan was smaller, tighter-knit, and more personal. Saipan's varied missions called for a mix of helicopters: CH-46 Sea Knight, giant CH-53 Sea Stallion, UH-1 Huey, AH-1 Super Cobra, and the AV-8 Harrier vertical-attack jet.

Six photographers manned the photo lab, and the mission was every bit as important. We supported Amphibious Forces,

Marine Units, and Photo Intelligence Operations, often in challenging environments that required flexibility, resourcefulness, and a deep understanding of the mission.

The work was hands-on and relentless. We documented Marine landing exercises, helicopter insertions, ship-to-shore operations, and amphibious training missions that simulated real-world combat scenarios. These weren't staged photo ops; they were rehearsals for amphibious landings or evacuations that could one day save lives. One opportunity occurred to photograph Navy SEALs training as they jumped from helicopters into the sea, capturing precision against the churn of rotor wash. The SEALs shared hair-raising stories of operations few would ever hear about. Those moments reminded me that behind every image was a story of courage, risk, and dedication.

Leading a small photo lab aboard Saipan presented a different kind of leadership challenge. With only six photographers, every sailor mattered, and teamwork was everything. I emphasized that photography is not just a skill, but a responsibility.

My time aboard Saipan also brought a milestone: I was promoted to Photographer's Mate Chief (PHC). It was a proud moment, my mother was aboard the Saipan to pin my Chief's anchors on my collar during the prestigious Chief Petty Officer ceremony. That new anchor symbolized more than seniority. It represented years of lessons learned, challenges overcome, and leadership attained. No longer just taking pictures, I was shaping how the Navy documented itself, guiding the next generation of photographers and preparing for whatever came next.

What came next was bigger than I could have imagined. My next orders had me reporting to Fleet Intelligence Center Europe and Atlantic (FICEURLANT), which we called it FIC. One of the Navy's most highly classified intelligence commands, responsible for imagery and intelligence operations across vast regions. It was a shift from my familiar world of photography into a more complex realm, satellite imaging intelligence.

At FIC, the stakes were higher and the work more sensitive than anything I'd done before. We processed satellite imagery for Admirals, the Joint Chiefs, and operations spanning the North Atlantic, the Mediterranean, and the Middle East.

The transition wasn't easy. I was surrounded by intelligence officers, analysts, and specialists whose language and methods were different. But I adapted as always. The same drive and discipline that drove me as a photographer motivated me in this new environment.

This assignment was intense, 24/7 Top Secret classified work in satellite image processing. After receiving Top Secret clearance to work at FIC, I returned to Pensacola, Florida, for a six-week course on the Kodak EH-38 Versamat processor. This training involved tearing down and rebuilding these machines. Through-out my career in photo labs, I had worked around these aerial processors but never trained to strip and rebuild them. The strict parameters for processing intelligence imagery required disciplined knowledge and the highest levels of continual quality control to ensure that imagery was never lost or degraded. This satellite imaging process was chemical-based and was later replaced by digital technology.

In 1989, I reached a defining milestone: I was commissioned as a Chief Warrant Officer Photographer (CWO2). Crossing over from the enlisted ranks to officer is one of the most significant transformations a sailor can make.  In the Navy, we call it becoming a Mustang, a term of deep respect because it means you've earned your commission through years of hard work, experience, and leadership from the deck plates up. The day my new rank was pinned on was one of the proudest moments of my career.

Before taking on my next assignment, I returned to Pensacola on TAD orders to attend Officer Indoctrination School, affectionately known in the Navy as "Knife and Fork School." The four-week course is designed to teach new officers how to lead, manage, and carry themselves with confidence and professionalism.  Sitting in those classrooms brought back memories of when my mother made me read Emily Post's book on Etiquette.  Mom's training allowed me to breeze through Knife and Fork School.

With Knife and Fork School complete, I was ready for the next chapter. My new orders would take me back to familiar waters, but in an entirely new role, returning to the *USS Dwight D. Eisenhower (CVN-69)*, not as an enlisted Photographer's Mate, but as the Division Officer and Photo Intelligence Officer. The ship and I had both changed since I first walked her decks in 1977.

*USS Saipan (LHA-2)*

*Captain C. Lind Re-enlists PHC (AW) Alleyne aboard the USS Saipan (LHA-2)*

*CWO2 Alleyne Re-enlists PH2 Tanner*

9

# Chapter 9

My Final Years in Uniform

*~ Fair Winds and Following Seas*

Reporting back to Eisenhower in 1989 brought back memories. The same decks where I once stood as a young Photographer's Mate now carried the weight of new responsibility and respect. This time, I would see the ship through a different lens, not from behind the camera, but from the leadership side of the frame. The faces were younger, the technology had evolved, and the Navy itself was entering a new era. Yet the sea, the hum of the engines, and the heartbeat of the crew were the same. I was no longer capturing the Navy's story; I was helping to write it.

This return marked the most defining moment of my career. As I stepped onto the quarterdeck, the ship's bell rang out in a time honored Navy tradition: "Plank Owner returning." That sound echoed deep within me.  It wasn't a ceremony; it was recognition, from the ship, the crew, and the sea itself, that this Plank Owner had been there at the very beginning, part of the team that brought the carrier to life. Now, I was returning as an officer to help lead her. It was one of the proudest moments of my life.

The ship had evolved since my first tour, and so had I. My responsibilities now reach far beyond the photo lab. I led both photographic and imagery intelligence operations aboard the carrier, ensuring our teams captured not only the ship's story but also the imagery needed for mission planning, analysis, and decision-making.

This second tour aboard Eisenhower, in 1990, placed me at the center of some of the most significant events of my career. The ship deployed through the Suez Canal to the Persian Gulf as part of Operation Desert Shield, a historic coalition effort to liberate Kuwait following Iraq's invasion. The tempo was intense, and the stakes were high as the ship operated as a ready striking force. Every launch and recovery on the flight deck, every briefing, every sortie carried weight. We documented it all, from flight operations over the Persian Gulf to the faces of the sailors and aviators who made history day by day.

It was during this deployment that I experienced one of the more unusual duties of my career:  serving as Beach Guard Officer during Eisenhower's port visits to Dubai, United Arab Emirates. When the ship anchored offshore and liberty boats ferried sailors to and from Fleet Landing.  I was part of a team in charge of the port landing operations, responsible for ensuring every sailor going ashore and returning to the ship did so safely and in accordance with Navy policy. It was a duty that demanded vigilance, diplomacy, and a steady hand, but it also offered a front-row seat to a part of deployment life most people never see.

Dubai itself was a fascinating port of call, a city on the cusp of transformation, where tradition and rapid modernization collided in striking ways. I will never forget Thanksgiving in Dubai. Despite being thousands of miles from home and in the middle of a major operation, the Navy made sure the holiday was memorable. Turkeys galore were served aboard ship, enough for 5,000 sailors, and for a few hours, the mess decks felt like home. Laughter echoed through the passageways, and the bonds forged during deployment felt even stronger that day.

This second tour on *IKE* was about more than missions and milestones. It was about legacy, watching young sailors grow into confident professionals, observing the ship I had helped commission over a decade earlier, carrying out operations on a global scale, and understanding more deeply how every image, every report, and every decision fit into the larger story of the Navy and its mission.

*IKE* returned in 1992 from a seven-month deployment in the Persian Gulf supporting Operation Desert Storm. The ship's crew was exhausted. As Naval operations around the world continued, a request for photo services came in for *IKE* to provide a photographer for an International Joint Exercise. It included a historic port call in which two U.S. ships, the USS *Yorktown* (CG-

*48)* and USS *O'Bannon (DD-987)*, visited Severomorsk, Russia, July 1-5, 1992, as part of a cultural exchange between the U.S. and Russian Navies. This was my final photo assignment, spending five days in Russia documenting ship tours, sporting events, Russian ballet, and dinners with Russian families. It was non-stop photography, requiring all of my photographic knowledge and know-how, from creating a makeshift photo lab on a ship without a darkroom for processing and printing, to providing the Admiral with souvenir photo albums. This endeavor required all of my photographic knowledge, from procurement to logistics. I needed to get photographic equipment to Norway, where the Admiral and staff would board the USS *Yorktown* (CG-48).

My most memorable interaction on this assignment was having lunch with a Russian naval officer and his family in their home. My thought was: here I am, a black naval officer, having a meal with a family whose country had been in conflict with mine throughout the Cold War. This cultural exchange gave me the once-in-a-lifetime opportunity to have an authentic Russian meal, starting with blinis as an appetizer, followed by Borscht soup. After lunch, I gave the family Polaroid pictures of our visit together. The father presented me with a book by the famous Russian author Anton Chekhov.

Closing out this assignment, I shot aerial photos of the USS *Yorktown* (CG-48) and the Russian Guided Missile Cruiser Admiral Levchenko in an Echelon formation. This 5-day trip to Russia has remained with me. The people, the country, and the Russian Navy provided a lifelong memory that the world can choose to co-exist in peace.

When the time finally came to leave Eisenhower at the end of my second tour, the tradition repeated itself. I was once again gonged off, this time as "Plank Owner departing." The sound of that bell carried twenty-two years of memories and nearly eight years of my life aboard a nuclear aircraft carrier. It symbolized not just the end of a chapter. Still, the completion of a journey, from an enlisted Photographer's Mate with a camera around his neck to a commissioned officer trusted with imagery that shaped operations. That farewell was bittersweet, but it filled me with immense pride. A few moments in my career matched the honor of that day. As I walked down the brow for the last time, saluting the ensign as a Naval officer, I realized something profound but straightforward. The sea had been my classroom, my test, and my teacher. The lessons I learned, and the images I captured, weren't just part of my career; they were part of me. They told the story of a life lived in uniform, surrounded by water, guided by purpose, and carried forward by the tide of time.

In 1993, I received my final set of orders: a transfer to Naval Submarine Base New London, Groton, Connecticut. It was a fitting last chapter, a chance to serve in an unknown photographic environment, the Submarine Force. Assigned to the Submarine Surveillance Equipment Program (SSEP). Contributing my experience to a new mission, the pace, was different, the challenges unique, but the commitment to excellence remained the high.

Submarine Base New London would be my twilight duty station, a quiet, focused base known as the "Home of the Silent Service." This assignment was different from anything I had done before. I had zero prior experience in the submarine world, but quickly adapted. Assigned to the Submarine Surveillance Equipment Program, I led a small group of Photographer's Mates responsible for periscope photography. Maintaining submarine periscope equipment, keeping it checked, preserved, and operational. I also served as Special Security Officer (SSO) for Submarine School, managing classified information and a Sensitive Compartmented Information Facility (SCIF) and materials.

The Navy had given me more than a career; it had given me purpose, discipline, and a worldview shaped by the sea. I had seen the world through the lens of service, from darkrooms to flight decks, from the calm of the Mediterranean to the heat of the Persian Gulf. When I finally stepped away from the sea, it felt like closing a book I had been writing my entire life, each chapter marked by ships, faces, and moments that tested and defined me. Yet, as any sailor knows, the horizon never truly ends. The lessons, friendships, and discipline that shaped me in uniform would guide the next course of my life ashore. My journey with the Navy had ended, but the story of what came after, the rediscovery of self and of life beyond the watch, was beginning.

*USS Yorktown (CG–48) & USS O' Bannon (DD–987)*

*Aerial Views of USS Yorktown (CG–48) & Admiral Levchenko
(DDG–605)*

# IV

# Part IV

*An Island Calls Again*

# 10

# Chapter 10

## Life After the Navy

*~ An unknown calling to a distant island*

In 1995, after twenty-five years in uniform, the Navy chapter of my life closed. It was a strange feeling to wake up without the 0600 sound of reveille, to put on civilian clothes instead of a uniform, and to know that no one would be saluting me. The Navy had shaped me, taught me discipline, leadership, and resilience. Stepping away from that life was both liberating and unsettling.

But my next mission was waiting for me, one rooted not in orders but in love and responsibility. I returned to Martha's Vineyard, the island where so many of my formative years had been spent. This time, I needed to care for my mother as her health began to decline. Becoming her caregiver was a different kind of duty, one that required patience, compassion, and presence. It was service, just in another form. While working, I cooked meals, managed her care, and simply sat and talked with her, grateful for every conversation. Those years deepened my understanding of family and reminded me that service doesn't end when the uniform comes off.

During that time, I began what became my second career, working for the island's Steamship Authority, the ferry line that connects Martha's Vineyard to the mainland. I started as a dockworker, docking boats and directing cars and trucks on and off the ferries. I later transitioned to the ticket office, where I sold ferry tickets and assisted with vehicle reservations. For seventeen years, I helped people cross the same stretch of water that had defined so much of my own life. Even without the Navy, I was still surrounded by water, just in a different way.

Life ashore had a slower rhythm, but the sea never left me. One day, while working on the docks, I noticed a fellow ferry employee wearing a gold shackle earring in his left ear. Curious, I asked where he'd gotten it. He told me a goldsmith in New Bedford custom-made them. That moment sparked a memory of Ed Bradley, the CBS pioneering Black journalist I'd long admired, who always wore a single earring. I decided it was time to get one myself, not as a fashion statement, but as a symbol.

In the Navy, a shackle is the link that connects the anchor to the chain, the vital link that holds a ship in place. I remembered reading that in the Bluejacket's Manual as a young sailor. One symbolic reason sailors wore earrings was to mark crossing the equator, something I had done more than once. So, I had a gold shackle earring made and placed it in my left earlobe. Since then, I've worn it every day. It's more than jewelry; it's a constant reminder of my life surrounded by water, a quiet tribute to where I've been, what I've carried, and the anchors that have held me steady through every tide.

About two years before my mother passed, I was hosting a backyard cookout with friends. As I stood by the grill, a guest walked over and complimented me on my home and yard. He said, "Tony, I know you've traveled the world, but have you ever been to Hawaii?" I told him I had been to Oahu, bustling and urban, reminding me of New York City, and I'd visited Kauai, which felt like Martha's Vineyard, quiet and rural. He asked, "Have you ever been to Maui?" I said no, I hadn't. He paused, smiled, and said, "Tony... you have not been to Hawaii." I laughed, unconvinced, and asked him what the heck he was talking about. His only reply was, "Once you go, you will know." I didn't realize just how much those words would shape my future. After my mother passed, those words came back to me with clarity. They weren't just about travel; they were about discovery, healing, and home.

So I went and visited, not knowing that Maui would become more than a destination. It would become home, the third island in my life's story, and the place where I would begin a new chapter surrounded by water once again.

Moving to Maui without knowing anyone was an adventure. I learned to experience a different rhythm. Life here unfolded at the pace of trade winds and tides. The light was softer, the days longer, and the ocean endlessly shifting and alive, never out of sight. After a lifetime of structure and schedules, I learned to move with the island instead of against it. I found beauty in simplicity: morning walks with the fragrance of Plumeria, sunsets that painted the sky in impossible colors, and stories that lingered as the waves rolled ashore.

Maui offered space to reflect and rediscover myself beyond the rank and ribbons. I returned to photography, but now it was a deeply personal way to capture the beauty around me and share the stories that had shaped me. The camera, once my tool of duty, became a companion of joy and curiosity.

Life on Maui also brought new relationships and new ways to contribute, small acts of connection that felt just as meaningful as the big missions had once been. It was here, in the middle of the Pacific, that I realized I wasn't leaving the sea behind. I was finally living with it.

Looking back now, I see my life as a journey across three islands, each one shaping me in unimaginable ways. Harlem, on the island of Manhattan, was my beginning, where resilience was forged, and dreams were born in the hum and rhythm of city streets. It taught me how to stand tall, how to navigate the noise, and how to believe in possibilities beyond my block.

Martha's Vineyard was my foundation, where I learned identity, purpose, and community. It was where my mother's strength anchored our family, where I grew into myself, and where I returned to serve again, this time not in uniform, but in love.

Maui is my reflection, where the pace slows, the water deepens, and I learn that legacy isn't about what you achieve but about how you live.  It's where I've found peace, connection, and meaning, and where I continue to write new chapters, even now.

Through it all, one constant has remained: water. It surrounded every chapter of my life, from the Hudson River to the Atlantic and Mediterranean Seas, from the waters around Martha's Vineyard to the vast Pacific.  It carried me across the world and always brought me home.  And like water, I've learned to move, to adapt, to carve my way through obstacles, and to reflect the life I've lived on the three M islands, Manhattan, Martha's Vineyard, and Maui.

I didn't plan this journey, not the Navy career, not the second career on the docks, not the gold shackle earring, and not the move to Maui. But every step, every sea, every island has brought me to this moment. My story isn't just about where I've been, it's about how islands shaped me, anchored me, and taught me to keep moving forward. I am, and always will be, surrounded by water.

*My Mother Audrey*

*My daughter Kimberly*

*Four Generations on Martha's Vineyard (L–R) Mother Audrey, Tony, Sister Vanessa, Daughter Kimberly, (Center) Nana Pansy*

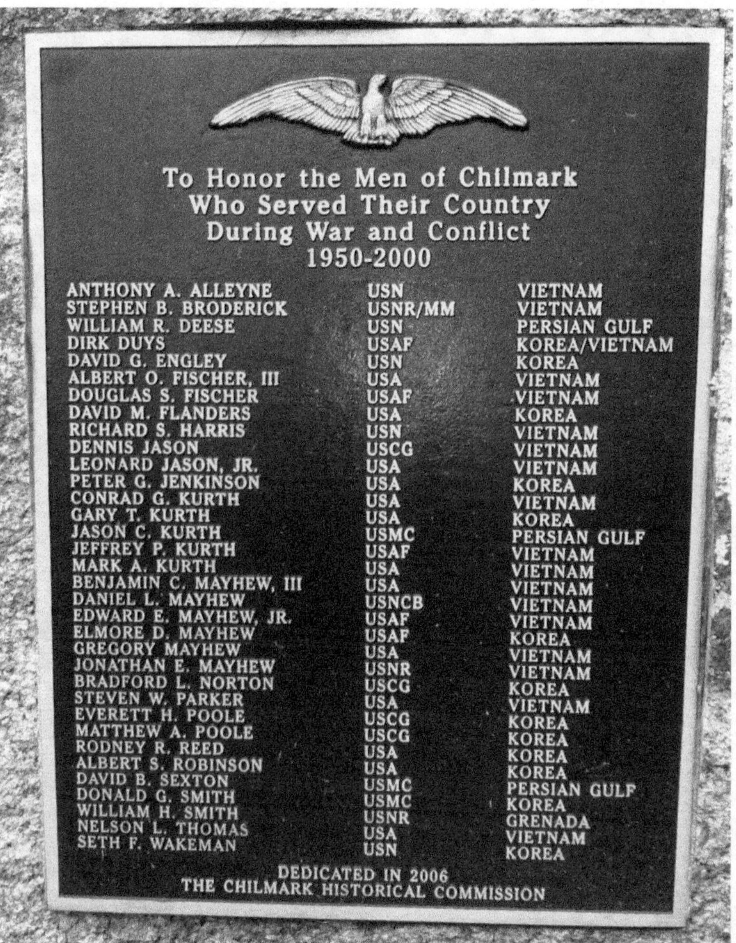

Town of Chilmark Plaque Honoring Men Who Served 1950 – 2000

*PH1 (AW) Anthony Alleyne*

# Epilogue

## The Horizon Beyond

The sea has always marked the passage of my life, each wave a memory, each tide a turning point. Looking back now, I see that my story was never just about service, duty, or travel. It was about learning how to navigate change, how to stand steady through storms, and how to find meaning in every new horizon.

The Navy gave me purpose, the islands gave me belonging, and time has given me perspective. I've seen the world from flight decks and ferries, from helicopters and quiet beaches. The people I served with, the places I've called home, and the images I've captured have been part of a larger journey toward understanding who I am and what truly matters.

Retirement hasn't meant slowing down; it's an intended reflection. The camera still finds its way into my hands, though now it captures sunsets instead of sorties, faces of friends instead of formal portraits. I live surrounded by water once more, listening to the same rhythm that has always guided me, steady and sure.

In the end, the measure of a life isn't found in medals, titles, or miles traveled, but in the memories you carry and the stories you leave behind. I've lived mine by the sea, learned from its patience and power, and found my peace within its endless embrace.

Wherever the next tide takes me, I'll be ready, because the sea, like life, always finds its way home.

# A Final Reflection



From the bustling streets of Manhattan, to the sandy beaches of Martha's Vineyard, and to the Spirit of Aloha on Maui, each island has offered me a different lesson. One taught me resilience. One taught me patience. One taught me when to listen, when to act, and when to let the tide carry me forward.

The sea has constantly reminded me that life moves in rhythms. There are times of motion and times of stillness. There are moments when you fight the current, and moments when you trust it. Every crossing, deployment, homecoming, and farewell taught me that growth arrives without fanfare.

I have stood on crowded city sidewalks and silent island shores. I have watched storms roll across open oceans and sunlight settle gently on calm harbors. Through it all, water has been integral in guiding me from one chapter of life to the next.

If these stories leave you with anything, I hope it is this: the places we pass through shape us, but they do not define our limits. Each of us carries within us the ability to adapt, to endure, and to begin again, no matter where the tide may take us.

My story is not just about islands, or ships, or years in uniform. It is about movement, memory, and meaning.  Learning to recognize the quiet currents that guide us all.

**Because in one way or another, we are all Surrounded By Water.**

# About the Author

Born into city life on one island, raised in country culture on another, and now retired on a multicultural island in the heart of the Pacific Ocean. Anthony Alleyne's life has been shaped by water, place, and the wisdom gained along the way.

Anthony Alleyne is a U.S. Navy veteran and the author of *Surrounded By Water Island Stories... Life on Three Islands.* He has lived and worked across three very different island communities, each leaving a lasting impression on his life and worldview.

With honesty and quiet reflection, he writes for readers who value real stories, meaningful journeys, and the strength found in lived experience. *Surrounded By Water* is his debut memoir and a tribute to the places, people, and moments that quietly shape who we become.